MW00897401

الله

Allah

The Only One God

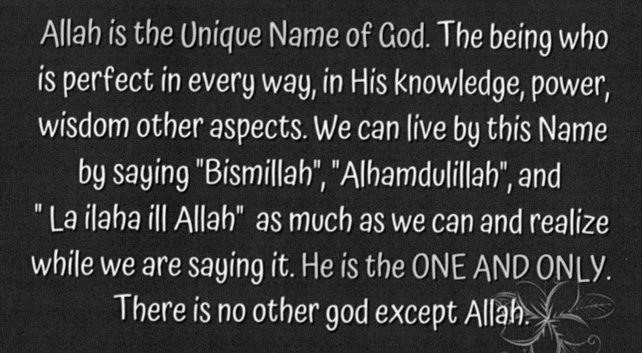

Allah is the Unique Name of God. The being who is perfect in every way, in His knowledge, power, wisdom other aspects. We can live by this Name by saying "Bismillah", "Alhamdulillah", and " La ilaha ill Allah" as much as we can and realize while we are saying it. He is the ONE AND ONLY. There is no other god except Allah.

الرَّحْمَنُ

1. Ar-Rahmaan

The Most Merciful

Allah is the most merciful to all mankind. Whenever we commit a sin. Call Him by His name to have mercy on you. How to live by this name, having mercy to people around us, especially family members, do not abandon them, and being grateful for what you have. Because all comes from Allah's mercy.

Quran: 41:2

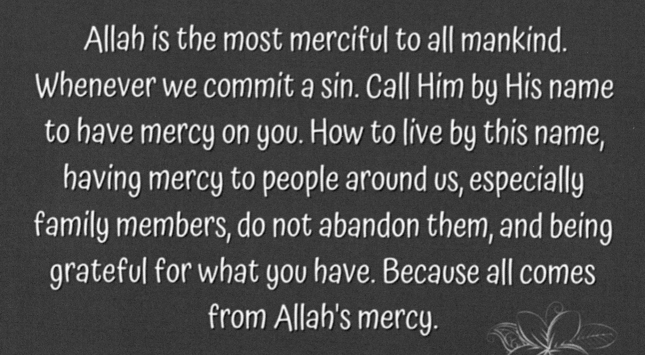

الرَّحِيمُ

2. Ar-Raheem

The Extremely Merciful

If we obey Allah and Messenger Muhammad peace be upon him (PBUH) and try our best to hold on to guidelines, prohibitions, and orders that are mentioned in the Quran and the Sunnah way. So that we surely receive mercy from Allah.

Quran: 12:98, 15:49, 26:9

الْمَلِكُ

3. Al-Malik

The King

Allah is The King, The One who rules the world and the whole universe. The heavens and the earth belong to Him. There is nothing above Him and He is alone that created the sun, trees, river, animals also us. All of these live under His rule and permission. We should thank Allah, for such incredible creations He makes.

Quran: 40:29

الْقُدُّوسُ

4. Al-Quddoos

The Most Holy/ Pure

Allah is free of any imperfection, and He is only the Perfect and Divine. We can apply Al-Quddoos by having pure belief in Allah, keeping ourselves clean away from sins, helping parents tidy up the house, and public areas. The most important is, always keep Quran purifying our hearts and souls.

Quran: 62:1

السَّلَامُ

5. As-Salaam

The Giver of Peace

Allah is The Giver of Peace. In our life, we can apply for as salaam in many ways. For example, by submitting in Islam so we can be surely secured by Allah, any time of troubles in our minds ask Allah for salaam then we will certainly feel peace in our hearts, and saying salaam to people we know and those we do not know, is one of the characteristics of being a good Muslim.

Quran: 36:57-58

الْمُؤْمِنِ

6. Al-Mu'min

The Giver of Faith and Security

Allah fills our hearts with faith that removes our fears. Whenever we feel insecure, have faith in Allah and ask Him for al-mu'min. Whoever has faith in Allah, also will receive His security. We should always thank Allah for the blessing of security and faith.

Quran: 59:23

الْمُهَيْمِنُ

7. Al-Muhaymin

The Ever-Watching

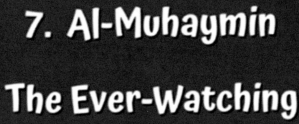

We should be thankful that Allah sees everything that we do all the time wherever we are, and at the same time, He knows what is good or bad for us. So if we need help or support, call upon Him. Then Allah will give it to us if we are patient.

Quran: 5:48

الْعَزِيزُ

8. Al-'Azeez

The All-mighty

Allah is strong and overpowers everything. All things around us in this world are made by His power. Even a small tiny thing or big mountain, no one can resist this power. So we should be confident and seek the power of Allah that everything can happen by His will. Whenever we feel weak or overpowered, turn ourselves to Allah. We will definitely receive his strength.

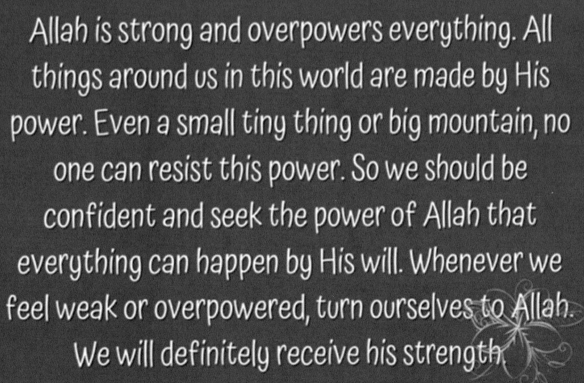

Quran: 3:26, 48:7

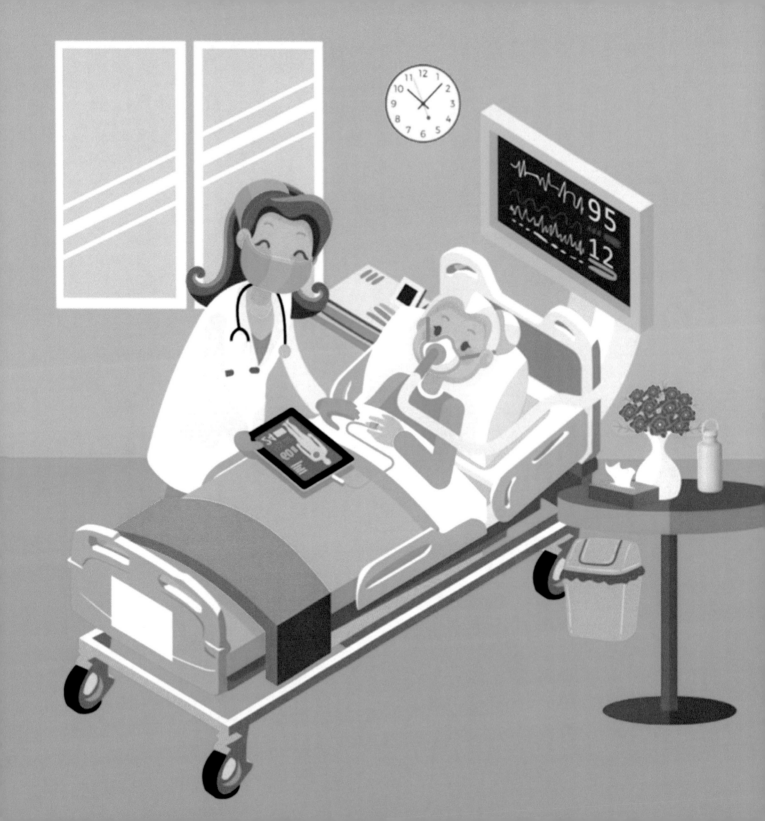

الْجَبَّارُ

9. Al-Jabbaar

The Restorer

Allah repairs everything around us and makes things right. Nothing happens without His Knowledge. He heals the brokenhearted, cures their wounds, and brings comfort to the weak. One of the types of al-jabbaar in our life is that we can practice mending someone's heart because Al-Jabbaar will mend yours in times of need.

Quran: 40:35

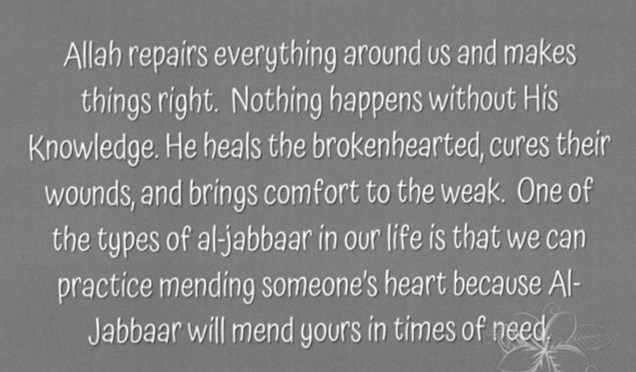

الْمُتَكَبِّرِ

10. Al-Mutakabbir

The Supreme

Allah is only good. We should apply al-mutakabbir in our life by, never being proud of ourselves, and never looking down upon other people. We should be humble towards our parents, and our teachers as they are good to us and give us knowledge. Also, ask Al-Mutabkabbir to save and protect us and our beloved ones in our life from the evil of pride and arrogance.

Quran: 4:27 , 3:160

الْخَالِقُ

11. Al-Khaaliq

The Creator

Allah creates absolutely everything, including people, animals, plants, buildings, food, and much more. One of the ways we can have khaaliq, if anything we desire, ask from The One who creates everything. Turn to Al-Khaaliq even for the smallest thing we need, because nothing is impossible with Allah.

Quran: 59:24, 25:86, 23:14

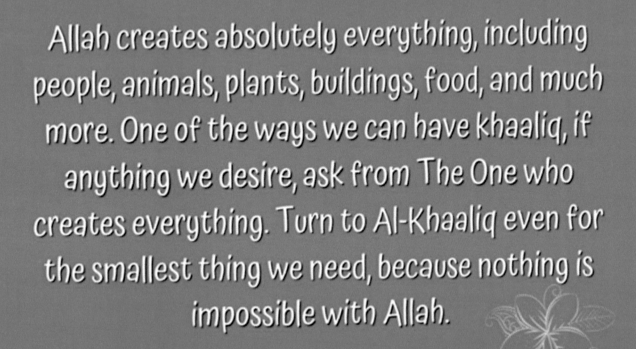

الْبَارِئُ

12. Al-Baari

The Maker / Originator

Allah was the first and the only one to make everything in this world. See! how things around us were made; for example, the sun, sky, sea... No human on earth can make them except Allah. Modern-day scientists want to make a fly and they are not able to. A fly is a complete living being with a tiny flight control system without turbines or propellers such a marvelous nano-technological design.

Quran: 95:4, 82:7, 27:88

الْمُصَوِّرُ

13. Al-Musawwir

The Shaper / The Fashioner

Allah was The One to give everything its shape and form. Look! how animals are shaped, all is from Allah's power. Everyone is beautiful and unique and all are made perfectly. We should not complain about our looks, just remember those who are blind, sick, and disabled. Moreover, Allah creates and differentiates us from animals, so use our hearing, sight, and hearts in the right way, not harm ourselves or others by sinning.

Quran: 59:24

الْغَفَّارُ

14. Al-Ghaffaar

The All-Forgiver

Allah is The All-Forgiver. He looks over our faults and sin over and over again, also protecting us from the outcomes of our mistake, for us to go on without shame or guilt in this life and the next. We should learn to forgive others and never hunt for others' mistakes. If we do something wrong we need sincerely ask forgiveness from Allah, and avoid repeating the same mistake and be thankful for this blessing.

Quran: 38:66, 40:42

الْقَهَّارُ

15. Al-Qahhaar

The Conqueror/ The Subduer

Allah is The Only One Subduer to all creations. Look! at how Al-Qahhaar commanded nature to change at His will. We can learn His power by the example of Noah's people. The great flooding washed away disbelievers and some of his family members of Noah who disbelieved in Islam. Islam means we submit and surrender to Al-Qahhaar.

Quran: 71:11

الْوَهَّابُ

16. Al-Wahhaab

The Giver of Gifts

Allah continually gives us everything including our family, home, toys, clothes, food, and much more things that make our life even more convenient. We should learn from this to give to others without expecting any in return. For instance, food, clothes and things that we do not need may benefit others. Besides, what Allah gifts you even a small thing, say thank you and use it in the right way.

Quran: 38:35

الرَّزَّاقُ

17. Ar-Razzaaq

The Provider

Allah provides His sustenance to all His creatures. There is no living creature on earth, except that Allah provides for it. Remember His providers can come from ways that we have never imagined. So be satisfied and grateful with all that we have been given, work hard on the right path, trust in Ar-Razzaaq, and never seek wicked means. Surely Allah will abundantly increase our provision for living.

Quran: 34:24, 67:21

الْفَتَّاحُ

18. Al-Fattaah

The Opener and The Judge

Allah opens up people's hearts to His path, and He opens the doors of mercy. When we are in difficult situations ask Him for a way out. We should always study Quran especially the first surah Al-Fatiha, the opening, learn to recite, memorize, and understand it. Life is full of arguments, but who is the judge? Of course Allah. If We are on the right side, do not be afraid, because Allah is Al-Fattaah is the just Judge. Also, we should not judge others too quickly.

Quran: 6:44, 34:26

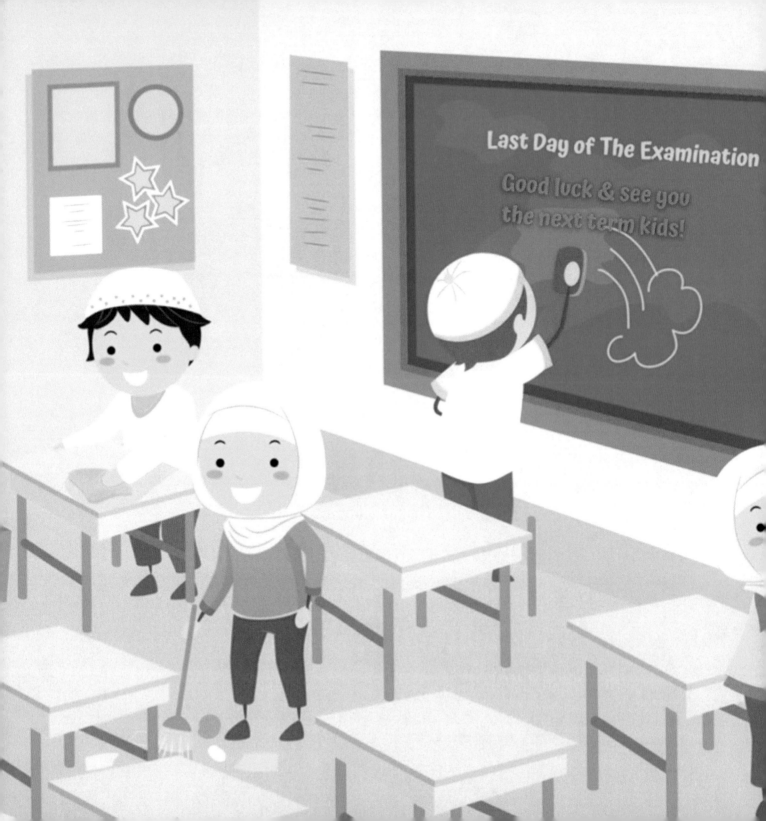

اَلْعَلِيْمُ

19. Al-Aleem

The All-Knowing

Allah sees, hears, and knows absolutely everything, which means He knows all of our secrets and even knows what we are thinking about. We can live by Al-Aleem asking Allah to increase our knowledge, especially in Islamic knowledge. Whenever being sick, stressed, or disappointed, remember Allah knows it very well. So be patient and ask Him to help you out. Be patient especially during these trials.

Quran: 66:2, 34:3

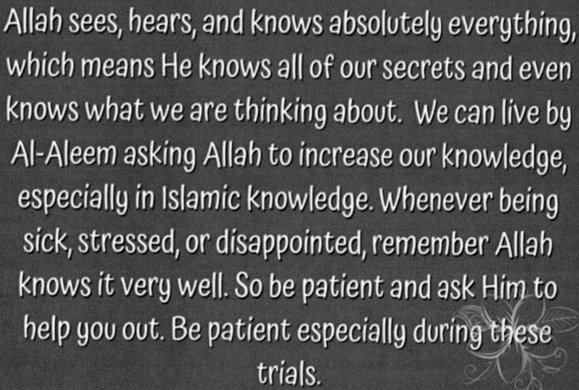

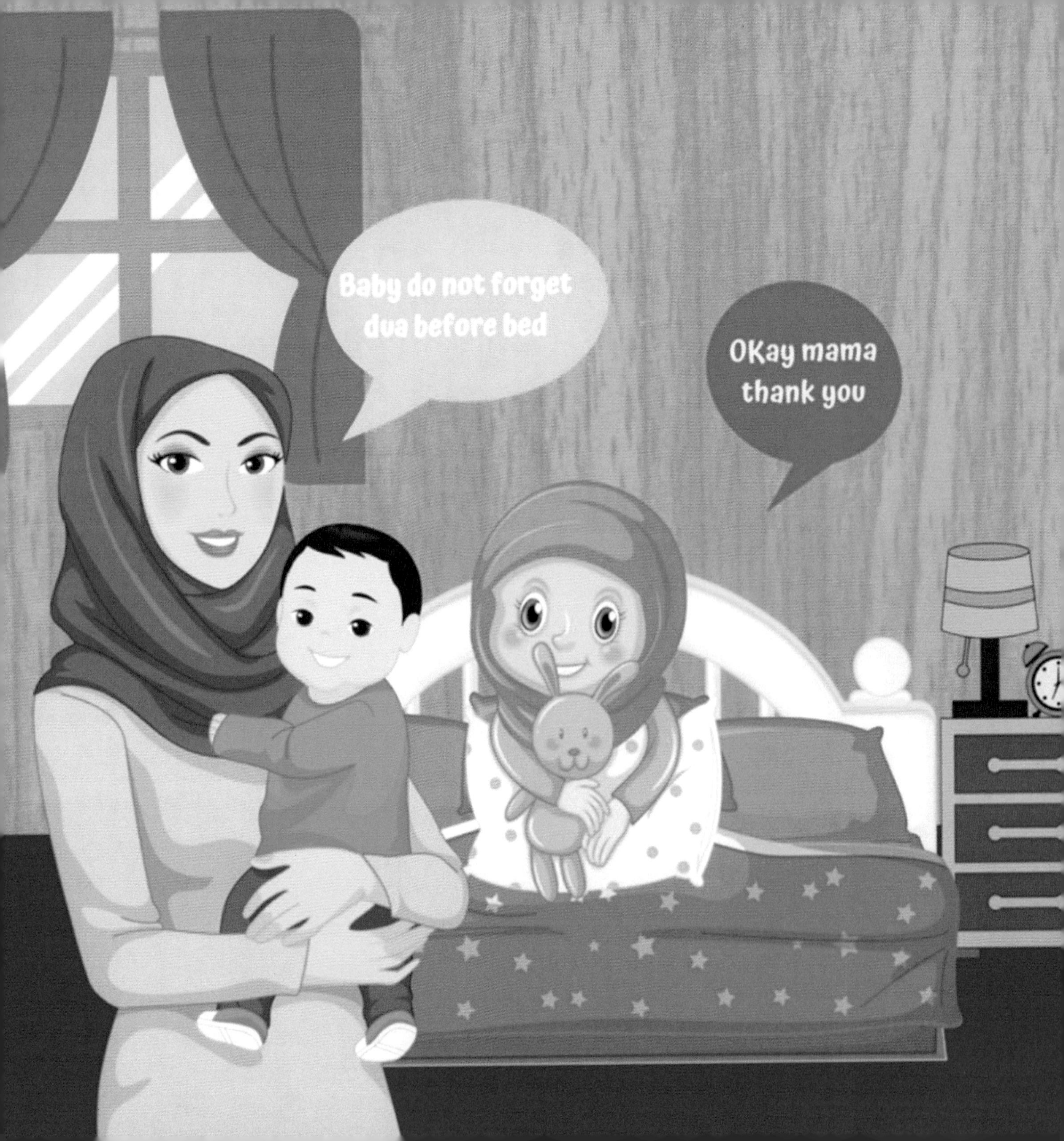
Baby do not forget dua before bed
OKay mama thank you

الْقَابِضُ

20. Al-Qaabid

The Taker

Allah decides to take something or makes something lacking. He is the taker of all souls at the time of death. The example of sleep in the name of Allah. When we sleep it's called a minor death, Allah takes the souls of some and they never wake up, or He returns the souls to them and they wake up. It is very important for us to make our bedtime dua before sleep.

Quran: 2:249, 13:26

الْبَاسِطُ

21. Al-Baasit

The Expander & Increaser

Allah increases all the good things that we have such as our living, knowledge, money, and faith to whomever He wills. In life, as long as we follow Allah's guidance, He will definitely increase His provision, blessings, and mercy to us. We should always be grateful to Allah for all ups and downs in our life. It can prove how faithful we are

Quran: 13:26, 42:47

الْخَافِضُ

22. Al-Khaafid

The Reducer

Allah is the one who brings down the prideful ones after giving them so many chances to change their ways. Also, Allah does the same to believers for testing their patience. As Muslims, we should be humble, obey Allah, avoid doing any major sins and stay patient in all situations. We will certainly receive a reward for hardship.

Quran: 56:3, 89:15-16

الرَّافِعُ

23. Ar-Raafi'

The Uplifter

Allah chooses who will be raised in a high position,
and Allah blesses and honors us because we are
Muslims. Thus, we should follow His path to satisfy
him, and do good deeds as much as we can.

Quran: 6:83, 95:4

الْمُعِزُّ

24. Al-Mu'izz

The Giver of Honor

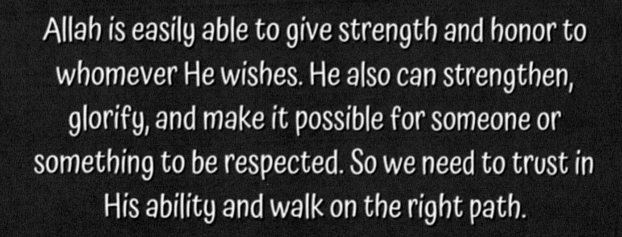

Allah is easily able to give strength and honor to whomever He wishes. He also can strengthen, glorify, and make it possible for someone or something to be respected. So we need to trust in His ability and walk on the right path.

Quran: 12:76, 35:10

ٱلْمُذِلُّ

25. Al-Muzil

The Giver of Dishonor

Allah creates the circumstance of dishonor and degradation, He gives respect to whomever He will, and there is no one to degrade Him. We should always obey Allah and His messager because if Allah dishonors anyone there will never be honored.

Quran: 57:14-15

Alhamdullilah

See You The Next Book!

References
The Noble Qur'an by Dr. Muhammad Taqi-ud-Din Al- Hilali & Dr. Muhammad Muhsin Khan
www.understandquran.com
www.questionislam.com
www.islamicreliefcanada.org
www.myislam.org

Made in the USA
Las Vegas, NV
22 April 2024

89002205R00033